A HISTORY OF RACISM IN AMERICA

Craig E. Blohm

San Diego, CA

About the Author
Craig E. Blohm has written numerous books and magazine articles for young readers. He and his wife, Desiree, reside in Tinley Park, Illinois.

© 2022 ReferencePoint Press, Inc.
Printed in the United States

For more information, contact:
ReferencePoint Press, Inc.
PO Box 27779
San Diego, CA 92198
www.ReferencePointPress.com

ALL RIGHTS RESERVED.
No part of this work covered by the copyright hereon may be reproduced or used in any form or by any means—graphic, electronic, or mechanical, including photocopying, recording, taping, web distribution, or information storage retrieval systems—without the written permission of the publisher.

Picture Credits:
Cover: Laurin Rinder/Shutterstock

4: Shutterstock.com
5: Shutterstock.com
8: Everett Collection/Shutterstock.com
12: Photo © CCI/Bridgeman Images
14: Bridgeman Images
17: Everett Collection/Shutterstock.com
22: Everett Collection/Shutterstock.com
25: Bridgeman Images

27: Peter Newark American Pictures/Bridgeman Images
31: Photo © Christie's Images/Bridgeman Images
33: Everett Collection/Shutterstock.com
37: Omniphoto/UIG/Bridgeman Images
41: Associated Press
43: Everett Collection/Bridgeman Images
49: Associated Press
52: Julian Leshay/Shutterstock
56: Associated Press

LIBRARY OF CONGRESS CATALOGING-IN-PUBLICATION DATA

Names: Blohm, Craig E., 1948- author.
Title: A history of racism in America / by Craig E. Blohm.
Description: San Diego, CA : ReferencePoint Press, Inc., 2022. | Includes bibliographical references and index.
Identifiers: LCCN 2021045475 (print) | LCCN 2021045476 (ebook) | ISBN 9781678201685 (library binding) | ISBN 9781678201692 (ebook)
Subjects: LCSH: Racism--United States--History. | United States--Race relations.
Classification: LCC E184.A1 B5595 2022 (print) | LCC E184.A1 (ebook) | DDC 305.800973--dc23
LC record available at https://lccn.loc.gov/2021045475
LC ebook record available at https://lccn.loc.gov/2021045476

CONTENTS

Important Events in the History of Racism in America   **4**

Introduction   **6**
The Idea of Race

Chapter One   **10**
Race and America's Beginnings

Chapter Two   **20**
Emancipation and Reconstruction

Chapter Three   **29**
Racism in the Early Twentieth Century

Chapter Four   **38**
The Civil Rights Era

Chapter Five   **47**
A New Century and an Old Problem

Source Notes   57
Organizations and Websites   60
For Further Research   62
Index   63

IMPORTANT EVENTS IN THE HISTORY OF RACISM IN AMERICA

1915
The film *The Birth of a Nation* becomes a hit and spurs the rebirth of the Ku Klux Klan.

1857
In the *Dred Scott* case, the US Supreme Court rules that Blacks do not have constitutional rights.

1619
First slaves from Africa arrive in Virginia.

1830
Indian Removal Act forces Native Americans to relocate from their ancestral lands.

1808
The United States officially bans the importation of slaves.

1700　1750　1800　1850　1900

1735
Swedish naturalist Carl Linnaeus categorizes races.

1863
President Abraham Lincoln signs the Emancipation Proclamation, which sought to free slaves in Confederate states but could not be enforced because those states had seceded from the Union.

1882
The Chinese Exclusion Act prohibits the immigration of Chinese laborers.

1896
In the case of *Plessy v. Ferguson*, the US Supreme Court rules that racial segregation is constitutional under the doctrine of "separate but equal."

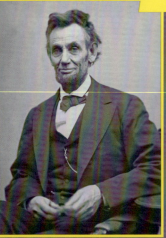

1954
In the case of *Brown v. Board of Education*, the US Supreme Court rules that segregated schools are unconstitutional.

2013
The Black Lives Matter movement forms in response to the acquittal of a Florida man who shot and killed an unarmed Black teenager.

1943
In Los Angeles, White military servicemen assault Hispanic teens in the zoot suit riots.

1919
Red Summer race riots create chaos across the nation.

1961
White supremacists in the South attack Freedom Riders as they try to desegregate public buses.

1940　　　1960　　　1980　　　2000　　　2020

1942
About 120,000 Japanese Americans on the West Coast are removed from their homes and interned in relocation camps.

1957
The Little Rock Nine break the color barrier in an Arkansas high school.

2020
The murder of George Floyd by a Minneapolis police officer leads to nationwide protests.

2021
Just over nine thousand racially motivated attacks on Asian Americans are reported from March 2020 to June 2021.

1948
President Harry S. Truman desegregates the US armed forces.

1922
In the case of *Ozawa v. United States*, Asian immigrants are ruled ineligible for citizenship in the United States.

INTRODUCTION

The Idea of Race

Scientists often categorize their findings in order to help bring a bit of order to the complicated world around us. Astronomers rank stars according to magnitude, or brightness; chemists add newly discovered elements to the periodic table; and biologists classify species according to their genetic composition. In the eighteenth century some scientists attempted to classify human beings according to their various physical characteristics, including skin color. Swedish biologist Carl Linnaeus proposed four categories of people based on race: Red, White, Yellow, and Black. Certain traits were associated with these groups. For example, Blacks were considered brutish and unintelligent, while Whites were regarded as smart and civilized.

There is only one problem with Linnaeus's method: the concept of using science as the basis of race is wrong. "Race is not biological. It is a social construct. There is no gene or cluster of genes common to all blacks or all whites,"[1] explains Angela Onwuachi-Willig, a professor at Boston University School of Law. All human beings, regardless of skin color, share the same genetic makeup. Describing race as a social construct means that it is a system created by society as a way of identifying people based on variations in skin color.

Without a scientific foundation, the meaning of race is fluid and can actually vary from society to society. "A person who could be categorized as black in the United States might be considered white in Brazil or colored in South Africa,"[2] says Onwuachi-Willig. In some contexts race may be a useful way of identifying people. Throughout history, however, it has been used to suppress those who appear different.

The Reality of Racism

For more than three hundred years beginning in the sixteenth century, Blacks were taken by force from their African homelands, herded into horribly overcrowded slave ships, and delivered to colonies in North America, to South America, and to the Caribbean islands. The Atlantic slave trade transported more than 12 million Africans to the region that came to be known as the New World. Nearly 2 million Blacks did not survive the voyages. Those who did were sold into servitude to labor on plantations, in mines, and as servants in the homes of rich planters. They were brutalized, whipped, and often killed by their masters.

In the aftermath of the Civil War, enslaved Blacks won their freedom, but life was little better than before the war. Although constitutional amendments were adopted to give freed slaves equality, Jim Crow laws in the South discriminated against Blacks in voting, employment, education, and public transportation. Fear that armed Blacks would turn on their former masters led to countless lynchings, which became public exhibitions attended by hundreds or thousands of White spectators.

Westward expansion, followed by industrialization, brought new insult to non-White populations. Native Americans were forcibly relocated to unfamiliar lands and their children sent away to boarding schools that would strip them of their cultural identity. In the mid-nineteenth century, immigrants from China came to America to find work on farms, in factories, in California's gold fields, and by building the transcontinental railroad. Other workers feared their successes and increasing numbers, leading to the 1882 law that prohibited future Chinese laborers from immigrating to the United States. Racism against Asians

> "Race is not biological. It is a social construct. There is no gene or cluster of genes common to all blacks or all whites."[1]
>
> —Boston University School of Law professor Angela Onwuachi-Willig

Black captives were forced to endure filthy, crowded, and often deadly conditions on ships that journeyed to the Americas. Once in port, the captives were sold into slavery.

continued into the twentieth century. Viewed as possible spies or saboteurs after the 1941 Japanese attack on Pearl Harbor, Japanese Americans living on the West Coast were rounded up and herded into relocation camps in isolated areas of the West. These American citizens lost their homes, businesses, and possessions while living in the camps.

The twenty-first century brought more ugly reminders of America's long and troubled relationship with race. Police killings of Black Americans, hateful rhetoric about people of Mexican descent, and racist attacks on Asian Americans signaled, once again, the need for a reckoning. At the instigation of the Black Lives Matter movement and others, systemic racism and racial injustice have moved to the forefront of national attention.

Good Trouble

Eliminating racism from American life is not a new goal. There is still a long way to go. But over time, there has been progress. In 1954 segregation in schools was ruled unconstitutional, giving millions of minority children access to a better education. In the 1960s legislation such as the Voting Rights Act of 1964 and the Civil Rights Act of 1965 became law, protecting minorities' constitutional rights. Protest marches, bus rides for freedom, sit-ins, and rallies in Washington, DC, all illuminated the challenges of racism in the United States.

With all the progress that has been made in combating racism, much still needs to be done. Racism is an ongoing problem that demands an ongoing solution. In a 2018 tweet, congressman and civil rights advocate John Lewis (who died in 2020) encouraged activists to continue their efforts for racial justice: "Be hopeful, be optimistic. Our struggle is not the struggle of a day, a week, a month, or a year, it is the struggle of a lifetime. Never, ever be afraid to make some noise and get in good trouble, necessary trouble."[3]

CHAPTER ONE

Race and America's Beginnings

"We hold these truths to be self-evident, that all men are created equal, that they are endowed by their Creator with certain unalienable Rights, that among these are Life, Liberty and the pursuit of Happiness."[4] These words, written by Thomas Jefferson in the Declaration of Independence, embodied the ideals and spirit of the new United States of America. In contrast to European monarchies, the new nation was based on the ideal of recognizing the equality of all people.

This ideal was rooted, in part, in the intellectual movement known as the Enlightenment. Beginning in eighteenth-century Europe, the Enlightenment emphasized rational and scientific thinking over the precepts of religion and faith. Numerous disciplines, such as chemistry, physics, biology, and mathematics, saw advances during the Enlightenment. Among the scientific efforts of the Enlightenment were attempts to more clearly understand the world by studying and classifying nature. This led to the classification of different races of people found around the globe. In 1735 Swedish naturalist Carl Linnaeus published a book called *Systema Naturae*, which categorized humans into four groups: Europaeus (White), Americanus (Red), Asiaticus (Yellow), and Africanus (Black). Such classification gave rise to a hierarchy of the various races (sometimes called scientific racism), ranking them according to assumptions about intelligence and moral values. Of Linnaeus's four groups, Blacks were considered inferior to the others.

> **"I am apt to suspect the negroes to be naturally inferior to the whites."[6]**
>
> —Scottish philosopher David Hume

Other Enlightenment intellects echoed Linnaeus's system. Immanuel Kant, a German philosopher, said, "Humanity exists in its greatest perfection in the white race."[5] Scottish philosopher David Hume, in his 1748 essay "Of National Characters," wrote, "I am apt to suspect the negroes to be naturally inferior to the whites. There scarcely ever was a civilized nation of any other complexion than white, nor even any individual eminent either in action or speculation. No ingenious manufactures amongst them, no arts, no sciences."[6]

The Enlightenment brought forth new ways of thinking about the world from the great minds of Europe. Despite Jefferson's elegant proclamation of equality for all, it was unavoidable that the Enlightenment, and the prejudices it encouraged, would cross the Atlantic and become a foundation for the new nation.

Early American Racism

By the late eighteenth century, America, liberated by revolution from a tyrannical king, had gained its independence and set forth a national framework in the US Constitution. But Blacks continued to be excluded from the benefits of liberty. Of the thirty-nine men who signed the Constitution, nearly one-third—including George Washington and James Madison—owned slaves. The Constitution does not specifically address slavery, but it declares that, of a state's population tallied for determining representation in Congress, only "three fifths of all other persons"[7] will be counted. Those "other persons" were slaves. Including enslaved Blacks, even though reduced to a fraction of a person, gave the southern states a larger voice in Congress and allowed the continued growth of slavery.

In 1790 the first US Census was taken. It revealed that, out of a population of some 3.8 million people in America, there were about 695,000 Black slaves. The Atlantic slave trade, which brought enslaved Africans to the Americas in appallingly overcrowded ships, flourished due to the need for Black laborers to work the southern plantations. About 10 million to 12 million enslaved Africans were shipped to the Western Hemisphere during the sixteenth to nineteenth centuries.

Although slave labor in the United States was primarily used in the agricultural South, all of the original thirteen states allowed some form of slavery. Most Blacks performed backbreaking labor on cotton, rice, and tobacco plantations. Others worked (and lived) in the master's house, cooking, cleaning, attending to the stables, and helping care for the master's children. Slaves were viewed as inferior to their White owners—and were treated that way. Daily life for the typical slave held fear and deprivation. The threat of physical punishment and even death hung over their lives for infractions both large and small. The vast majority had little chance for any education, no real health care, and inadequate food and shelter. Slaves were property to be bought and sold like cattle, often separated from their families. The cruelest separations occurred when children were taken from their parents. Former slave Henry Bibb described such a scene: "The child was torn from the arms of its mother amid the most heart-rending

An overseer on horseback watches Black slaves picking cotton. Many slaves did backbreaking work in the fields found on cotton, rice, and tobacco plantations. Others worked in the master's house or stables.

shrieks from the mother and child on the one hand, and the bitter oaths and cruel lashes from the tyrants on the other."[8] The chance of a slave family being reunited after its members were sold to various owners was nearly nonexistent.

Native Americans and White Suppression

Black people in America were not the only group viewed through the lens of racism. When the first European colonists landed in the New World, they were greeted by Native Americans, a people that had inhabited the continent for more than fifteen thousand years. The Native people initially helped the newcomers as they struggled to survive in a harsh and unfamiliar land. But the relationship turned hostile as the colonists began acquiring Native American land. The Europeans had no qualms about confiscating these territories; they considered the Native inhabitants to be inferior, their concept of the natural world unscientific, and their religion ripe for conversion to Christianity. The colonists believed themselves destined to remake the world in their own image. Colonial leader Thomas Paine declared in his 1776 pamphlet *Common Sense*, "We have it in our power to begin the world over again. . . . The birthday of a new world is at hand."[9] That new world would be defined by White males of European descent.

An adherent to this philosophy, Jefferson envisioned that Native Americans would turn away from their own indigenous culture and become assimilated into what he considered to be the enlightened European way of life. He hoped they would learn English methods of farming and adopt a less nomadic society. To help accomplish this, in 1819 the Civilization Fund Act established a partnership between the federal government and Christian missions. This act financed boarding schools in which native children were assimilated, or taught to live according to the rules of White society. They were forbidden to speak their own language or

> "We have it in our power to begin the world over again. . . . The birthday of a new world is at hand."[9]
>
> —Colonial leader Thomas Paine

wear native clothing, and they were given Anglo names to replace their native names. Long hair, a symbol of Native American identity, was cut short. Attendance at the schools was required, and many children were forcibly separated from their families. Some parents hid their children from the authorities, and many fathers went to jail for trying to obstruct the system.

Attitudes toward Native Americans hardened in the southeastern states after 1803. That year the United States purchased some 827,000 square miles (2,142,000 sq. km) of land from the Mississippi River to the Rocky Mountains. Called the Louisiana Purchase, it doubled the land area of the United States. With this land acquisition, the United States now had a place to send the unwanted Native Americans. In 1830 legislation called the Indian Removal Act authorized the US government to relocate native tribes to land west of the Mississippi, a region that became known as Indian Territory. Treaties signed by both parties were frequently unfavorable to the Native Americans, negotiated in bad faith by US Indian agents who often used deceitful methods and terms that the Native people did not fully understand.

The most brutal act of removal took place in 1838, when the US Army forced some sixteen thousand Cherokee men, women,

Native American children attend class at Carlisle Indian School in 1901 in Pennsylvania. Thousands of Native American children were forced to attend boarding schools that sought to strip them of their cultural identities.

Life in an Indian Boarding School

Mary Annette Pember's mother, Bernice, attended Saint Mary's Catholic Indian Boarding School on the Ojibwe reservation in Odanah, Wisconsin. The pain of that experience affected both her and her family. In an article for the *Atlantic* magazine, Pember relates what life in these schools was like for her mother and for thousands of other young Native Americans.

> Students were stripped of all things associated with Native life. Their long hair, a source of pride for many Native peoples, was cut short, usually into identical bowl haircuts. They exchanged traditional clothing for uniforms, and embarked on a life influenced by strict military-style regimentation. Students were physically punished for speaking their Native languages. Contact with family and community members was discouraged or forbidden altogether. Survivors have described a culture of pervasive physical and sexual abuse at the schools. Food and medical attention were often scarce; many students died. Their parents sometimes learned of their death only after they had been buried in school cemeteries, some of which were unmarked.

Mary Annette Pember, "Death by Civilization," *The Atlantic*, March 8, 2019. www.theatlantic.com.

and children from their homeland in the Southeast to the territory that is now Oklahoma. During the trek known as the Trail of Tears, an estimated four thousand people died of disease, starvation, and exposure to the elements.

Racism Against Hispanics

The mid-nineteenth century marked the start of racial turmoil for other groups as well. The 1848 Treaty of Guadalupe Hidalgo, which ended a two-year-long conflict called the Mexican-American War, gave territory that had been held by Mexico to the United States. Hispanics living there were promised they could keep their land, but they had to show proof of ownership, something Mexico had not required. Land disputes were brought to court, often resulting in lengthy and costly trials. Hispanics who could not prove their property ownership had their land seized by the government. Those who won their cases kept their land but were often impoverished by heavy legal fees.

The California gold strikes of 1848 attracted thousands of Hispanics west to work the gold fields. They soon clashed with local Whites, who considered the newly arrived Brown workers inferior and lazy. Other points of contention between Whites and the newcomers were the ethnic customs the Hispanics practiced, their Catholic religion, and the fact that they did not speak English.

Hispanics were soon burdened by unfair laws and taxes. Many Hispanics took up farming and ranching to make a living. A tax on farmland and a miners' tax that charged twenty dollars a month for the right to mine placed heavy burdens on Hispanic immigrants. In 1855 California passed an anti-vagrancy law that mainly targeted Hispanics who could not find work, subjecting them to fines or imprisonment. The law was known as the "Greaser Law," using a derogatory epithet for a Hispanic person.

Auctions and Rebellion

While Hispanic immigrants were fighting to keep their farms and ranches, most Native Americans had been removed from their ancestral lands, and farmers in the southern states could now expand their plantations. The growth of plantations made slave labor even more valuable to the southern economy. In 1850 there were about 3.2 million enslaved Blacks in the nation. Even though the importation of slaves was officially ended in 1808, buying and selling of enslaved Africans within the states continued. Slave auctions were an almost daily occurrence; Blacks were held in pens or jails until brought to be sold at auction houses, at railroad stations, on courthouse steps, and in taverns, among other locations. The auctions tore families apart, separating husbands from wives and babies from their mothers. The anguish of the slave auction was recalled by an Arkansas woman, Will Ann Rogers: "When Ma was a young woman, she said they put her on a block and sold her. . . . Her mother fainted or dropped dead, she never knowed which. She wanted to go and see her mother lying over there on the ground, and the man what bought her wouldn't let her. He just took her on. Drove her off like cattle, I reckon."[10]

Many slaves tried to escape their servitude, but the law was against them. The 1793 Fugitive Slave Act decreed that any slaves who ran away from their masters could be captured and returned to their owners. Penalties were also levied on those who helped a slave escape. Northern antislavery states opposed this law and rarely enforced it. As opposition grew, a new fugitive law was passed in 1850, making it even harder for slaves to escape to freedom.

Many enslaved Africans took great risks to fight back against the horrors of their servitude. In August 1831 a Virginia slave named Nat Turner felt that God had called him to eradicate slavery. He led a rebellion against slave owners in which some fifty-five Whites were killed. The rebellion was ultimately suppressed. Turner and more than fifty of the other rebels were executed by

Nat Turner, a Virginia slave, led a rebellion that resulted in dozens of deaths—including his own. A nineteenth-century engraving depicts Turner's capture.

Slavery in a Free Nation

It seems ironic that many of the men who founded a nation where "all men are created equal" owned slaves. George Washington, Thomas Jefferson, James Madison, John Hancock, and other founders owned slaves at one time or another. "How is it that we hear the loudest yelps for liberty among the drivers of negroes?" asked British writer Samuel Johnson in 1775.

By the beginning of the American Revolution, slavery in the colonies had been an established institution for more than a century. In the farm-based economies of the South, slavery was considered an unfortunate but necessary institution. In the industrial North, few people owned slaves but Northerners also benefitted from their labor.

Opinions, however, were beginning to change as the new nation sought independence. Jefferson (who is said to have owned six hundred slaves over his lifetime) included an antislavery passage in his first draft of the Declaration of Independence. In it, he denounced slavery and the transatlantic slave trade. Due to economic and political pressures from southern colonies, the passage was removed from the final Declaration of Independence. Thus, America's most important founding document was silent on slavery, allowing it to shape the future of the new nation.

Quoted in Mark Maloy, "The Founding Fathers Views of Slavery," American Battlefield Trust, 2021. www.battlefields.org.

state officials, with hundreds more beaten by civilian mobs or militia. As a result of the rebellion, fear of similar violence by Blacks spread throughout the South and caused southerners to pledge revenge for future rebellions. An anonymous letter published in October 1831 in the *Christian Register* newspaper vowed, "Another such an attempt [at rebellion] will end in the total extermination of their race in the southern country. . . . Bloody as the remedy may be, it will be better thus to rid ourselves of, than longer endure the evil."[11] Southern lawmakers also passed new laws that prohibited educating slaves and restricted religious observances and other constitutional freedoms.

Not Entitled to Freedom

The new laws brought added restrictions on Black residents in various southern states. These and other similar laws gained institutional status in 1857. That year, in a landmark decision, the US Supreme Court essentially ruled that racism against Black people was supported by the Constitution. The ruling came in a case brought by Dred Scott, a Black man who was born a slave in Virginia and later moved with his owners to Missouri. Sold to a new master, Scott was again relocated, first to the free state of Illinois and then to the free Wisconsin Territory. Moving back to Missouri in 1846, Scott sued to obtain his freedom, arguing that he had become a free man by virtue of his previous stays in free areas. Scott lost his bid for freedom in the Missouri courts, so he took his case to the Supreme Court.

Scott's case for freedom came before the high court in March 1857. Chief Justice Roger B. Taney was sympathetic to the southern cause and the institution of slavery. The rest of the court was inclined to support slavery: seven of the nine justices had been appointed by presidents with a bias toward slavery. In a 7–2 decision, the court decided that Scott was not entitled to his freedom even though he had spent time in free territory. The ruling stated that people of African descent "are not included, and were not intended to be included, under the word 'citizens' in the Constitution, and can therefore claim none of the rights and privileges which that instrument provides for and secures to citizens of the United States."[12] Thus, enslaved Africans had no constitutional right to claim their freedom, since they were not considered citizens of the United States.

Dred Scott was ultimately emancipated by his owner a few months after the Supreme Court's decision. But he did not enjoy his freedom for long. He died at age fifty-nine in September 1858.

The *Dred Scott* decision inflamed a nation already divided into a proslavery South and an antislavery North. Within a few years, the two sides would be engaged in the bloodiest war in American history, a conflict that would determine the fate of slavery in the United States.

> "[Blacks] are not included, and were not intended to be included, under the word 'citizens' in the Constitution, and can therefore claim none of the rights and privileges which that instrument provides for and secures to citizens of the United States."[12]
>
> —*Dred Scott* decision, US Supreme Court

CHAPTER TWO

Emancipation and Reconstruction

Fearing that their slave-based economy and way of life would be ended by the growing abolitionist sentiment in the rest of the nation, eleven Southern states seceded from the Union and in 1861 formed the Confederate States of America. The Confederate siege of Fort Sumter in April 1861 began four years of terrible fighting and appalling losses, of Americans killing Americans in support of opposing ideals.

Although morally opposed to slavery, newly elected president Abraham Lincoln saw preservation of the Union as his primary responsibility. Thus, he did not initially make any effort to end slavery. "I have no purpose," he said in his first inaugural address, "directly or indirectly, to interfere with the institution of slavery in the States where it exists."[13] Not everyone in the North shared Lincoln's viewpoint, however. Abolitionists were people who strongly advocated for the end of slavery and the punishment of Southern slaveholders, and their numbers were steadily increasing.

Growing pressure on Lincoln convinced him to change his thinking on slavery. In September 1862 he issued a warning to the South in the form of a preliminary Emancipation Proclamation. It declared that if the South did not cease hostilities by the end of 1862, all slaves in the states that had seceded would be emancipated, or freed. When the new year came with no change in Confederate belligerence, the Emancipation Proclamation went into effect. The proclamation did not, however, free any slaves. Since it applied only to the states that had left the Union, Lincoln had no authority to enforce its provisions. Fearing that the Emancipation Proclamation might be overturned after the war, Lincoln supported a proposed constitutional amendment that would ban slavery for good. The Thirteenth Amendment was sent to the states for ratification in February 1865 and finally adopted in December of that year.

> "I have no purpose, directly or indirectly, to interfere with the institution of slavery in the States where it exists."[13]
>
> —US president Abraham Lincoln

The Civil War ended in 1865. The North emerged victorious, and the South, now without slavery, was left in ruins, its economy a shambles. All across the South, bitter feelings against the North prevailed. "We had all our earnings swept away," wrote an Alabama farmer's wife. "The Government of the United States has the credit of giving the black man his freedom, while it was at the expense of the Southern people."[14]

Lincoln's postwar plan included amnesty for the states that had seceded. But on April 14, five days after the South surrendered, Lincoln was assassinated by Southern sympathizer John Wilkes Booth. The man who had promised in his second inaugural address to "bind up the nation's wounds"[15] was gone, and a new president would have to deal with the aftermath of the war and the racial attitudes that still existed.

Reconstruction in the South

With the end of the Civil War and the death of Lincoln, America entered a period called Reconstruction. Guiding Reconstruction was Andrew Johnson, a former slave owner from Tennessee who, as vice president, succeeded Lincoln to the presidency. Johnson believed in the superiority of the White race. His plan for reuniting the nation included pardoning former Confederate officers and instituting White-controlled state governments in the South. Congress authorized federal troops to occupy the former Confederate states until their new governments could be formed.

In 1862 President Abraham Lincoln and his Cabinet hear a first reading of the Emancipation Proclamation. Although the proclamation did not actually end slavery in America, it signaled for the first time that eliminating slavery was a goal of the Union.

As these governments were established, they endeavored to preserve a society in which Blacks remained submissive to Whites. New state constitutions reflected this attitude, as South Carolina's governor Benjamin F. Perry proclaimed in 1865: "This is a white man's government, and intended for white men only."[16]

Opposing such racial oppression was a group of legislators in Congress called the Radical Republicans. They believed that Blacks should have the same freedoms as Whites, and they enacted legislation to achieve this goal. When Congress passed the Civil Rights Act of 1866 (overriding Johnson's veto), all people born in the United States became citizens regardless of race and received guarantees of their civil rights. The Fourteenth Amendment, ratified in 1868, strengthened the guarantees of the Civil Rights Act, and the Fifteenth Amendment in 1870 declared that no citizen could be deprived of the right to vote based on "race, color, or previous condition of

> "This is a white man's government, and intend for white men only."[16]
>
> —South Carolina governor Benjamin F. Perry

servitude."[17] *Citizen*, in the 1870s, referred only to men. American women did not win the right to vote until 1920.

Black codes, sometimes called Black laws, were enacted by southern states after the war to nullify the advances for Blacks that Reconstruction afforded. Under these laws, freedmen could not serve on juries in cases involving White defendants, own firearms, or send their children to school. They were required to sign annual labor contracts with their employers, often the masters they had worked for as slaves. Freedmen without jobs or a permanent residence were considered vagrants, who could be arrested, fined, and forced to work until their fines were paid. The Black codes were enforced by White militias, many of which included former Confederate soldiers.

Although the Fifteenth Amendment assured Black men of equal voting rights, the Black codes circumvented that by placing restrictions on Black voters. One such restriction, for example, allowed Blacks to vote only if an ancestor had voted before 1867. But since at that time most Blacks were not allowed to vote, the law made it impossible for most Black men to vote. Literacy tests were imposed on both Black and White voters, but Whites received an easy test while Blacks had to take a particularly difficult test, which few, if any, could pass.

With the removal of federal troops that had been keeping order in the southern states, Reconstruction ended in 1877. Black southerners found themselves in circumstances that were little better than before the war. But life for freedmen was about to get even worse as violent groups sprang up across the South.

Hate Groups in the Postwar South

Despite the constitutional guarantees of equality for all, many people in the South were unwilling to abandon the antebellum, or pre–Civil War, social order that had kept Blacks subservient. White supremacists organized hate groups to terrorize and intimidate newly emancipated freedmen. In 1865 a group of former Confederate officers established one of the most violent of these groups.

Abolitionist Frederick Douglass

The abolitionist movement of the nineteenth century was dedicated to the immediate ending of slavery in the United States. Both Black and White activists worked toward this goal. One of the most prominent Black abolitionists was a former slave named Frederick Douglass.

Born into servitude around 1818 in Maryland, Douglass taught himself to read and write, and he taught other slaves as well. He eventually escaped to freedom in New York City. After marrying and moving to Massachusetts, Douglass attended abolitionist meetings and toured the country with the American Anti-Slavery Society, spreading the message of abolition. He also published an abolitionist newspaper called the *North Star* and wrote several autobiographies. Douglass was an advisor to Abraham Lincoln, urging the president to allow Blacks to serve in the Union army.

Of slavery, Douglass said, "The American people have this to learn: that where justice is denied, where poverty is enforced, where ignorance prevails, and where any one class is made to feel that society is an organized conspiracy to oppress, rob, and degrade them, neither person nor property is safe." Frederick Douglass died in 1895, forever remembered as a hero who fought slavery with pen and voice.

Quoted in Jennifer M. Wood, "20 Powerful Quotes from Frederick Douglass," *Mental Floss*, February 14, 2018. www.mentalfloss.com.

Called the Ku Klux Klan (KKK), its aim was to intimidate Blacks who were now allowed to vote and hold political office. Whites who supported the advances made by Blacks were also targeted. Led by former Confederate general Nathan Bedford Forrest, the KKK began a reign of terror, beating and murdering freedmen, destroying property (including schools and churches), and threatening future violence. Klan members held secret meetings and conducted horseback raids at night, wearing disguises to hide their identities. During these midnight rides, hooded Klansmen often pretended to be the ghosts of Confederate soldiers to further instill fear in superstitious and largely uneducated Blacks. Local White law enforcement officers turned a blind eye toward the KKK's campaign of terror and seldom prosecuted Klan members.

As the 1868 presidential election approached, Klan violence increased against people who were likely to vote Republican, the party favoring Black equality. This included newly enfranchised Black voters. In Louisiana, for example, about one thousand

Blacks were murdered before the election. Despite such intimidating violence, the Republican candidate, former Union general Ulysses S. Grant, was elected president.

By 1870 local chapters of the KKK were active in almost all the southern states. Other racist groups, such as the Knights of the White Camelia and the Order of the Pale Faces, also conducted terror campaigns against Blacks and their supporters. But as the twentieth century approached, the KKK and other White supremacist groups began losing their vindictive power. This was due to southern states enacting new laws that codified efforts to keep racism alive by legal means.

Jim Crow and a Landmark Decision

In the 1880s more laws were passed in southern states to further limit the rights of Blacks. Known as Jim Crow laws (named for an offensively stereotyped Black character played by a White actor wearing blackface in popular minstrel shows), these ordinances

In 1943 passengers come and go outside the clearly labeled "White Waiting Room" at a Greyhound bus terminal in Memphis, Tennessee. Jim Crow laws forced Blacks to use separate facilities, including restrooms, water fountains, and waiting rooms.

The Chinese Exclusion Act

In the nineteenth century a growing sentiment that Chinese laborers were taking jobs away from White workers fueled fierce anti-Chinese prejudice. In 1882 President Chester A. Arthur signed into law the Chinese Exclusion Act, which prohibited the immigration of all Chinese laborers into the United States. The small number of Chinese non-laborers who sought to immigrate to the United States had to prove they were not laborers, a task made so difficult that few could qualify.

The law prompted Whites on the West Coast to expel Chinese people from their towns. Some three hundred of these purges took place, one of the worst occurring in 1885 in Tacoma, Washington. A White mob marched through the city's Chinatown area, going house to house and forcing residents to leave town. Some two hundred men, women, and children had to walk through rain and mud to reach a train station, where they boarded a train to Portland, Oregon.

The Chinese Exclusion Act was the first US law to effectively ban an entire race of people from entering the country. Initially planned to last for ten years, the law remained in effect until 1943. That year Chinese immigration resumed, but even then only about one hundred Chinese were allowed to enter the United States annually.

further separated Blacks from White society. Jim Crow laws barred Blacks from using White restrooms, required separate Black railroad cars and waiting rooms, and created segregated Black sections in restaurants and theaters. Blacks were forbidden to marry outside of their race. Segregation even reached beyond the grave: Blacks could not be buried in White cemeteries. Jim Crow laws kept Blacks as second-rate citizens. These laws would soon be challenged in the courts but, initially at least, to no avail.

In 1892 a Black man named Homer Plessy challenged segregation by deliberately sitting in a Whites-only railroad car. He was arrested, and his case, entitled *Plessy v. Ferguson*, went all the way to the Supreme Court. In a landmark decision in 1896, the court declared that "separate but equal" facilities for Blacks did not violate the Constitution. In reality, such equality was a myth: the facilities that Blacks were forced to use were dirty and poorly maintained compared to White facilities. "Travel in the segregated South for black people was humiliating," writes human rights activist Diane Nash. "The very fact that there were separate facilities was to say to black people and white people that blacks were so subhuman and so inferior that we could not even use the public facilities that white people used."[18]

The decision in *Plessy v. Ferguson* that segregation was legal allowed a society of toxic racism to endure for nearly sixty years. The ruling was finally judged unconstitutional in 1954.

> "The very fact that there were separate facilities was to say to black people and white people that blacks were so subhuman and so inferior that we could not even use the public facilities that white people used."[18]
>
> —Human rights activist Diane Nash

Racism Against Asians

By the time of the original Supreme Court ruling in the *Plessy* case, racial discrimination against other groups was already well established in the United States. Rapid westward expansion in the 1850s required new sources of cheap labor to work in the mines and gold fields of California and on the Central Pacific Railroad, the western leg of the growing transcontinental railroad. Fleeing economic chaos in their homeland, thousands of Chinese immigrants flooded

A newspaper illustration depicts an 1880 anti-Chinese riot in Denver, Colorado. In various parts of the West around this time, Chinese workers were beaten by mobs, cheated out of wages, and driven from their homes by vigilantes.

into the American West. But with jobs in a White society came racism against the Chinese workers. In a study of Asian immigration published in the journal *Justice Quarterly*, the authors state, "In the nineteenth century, Chinese immigrants were stereotyped as degraded, exotic, dangerous, and perpetual foreigners who could not assimilate into civilized western culture."[19] Chinese workers were beaten by mobs, cheated out of fair wages, and driven from their homes by vigilantes who feared the Chinese would take their jobs. In a two-hour spree of deadly violence in 1871, a mob of some five hundred vigilantes tortured, shot, and hanged nineteen Chinese people in the Chinatown section of Los Angeles. Eight of the perpetrators were arrested and convicted of manslaughter, but all were freed within a year.

Anti-Coolie clubs, named for a racial slur for an unskilled Asian laborer, sprang up in many areas of California. These organizations spoke out against Chinese immigration. They also supported deportation of immigrant workers, who employers preferred to hire over White laborers because they worked for lower wages. In 1862 the California legislature passed the Anti-Coolie Act (also known as the Chinese Police Tax), which levied a monthly tax on each Chinese laborer. The tax was eventually struck down by the California Supreme Court, which ruled it unconstitutional.

West Coast newspapers also helped spread hostility toward Asians. Andrew King, editor of the *Los Angeles News* from 1865 to 1870, incited anti-Chinese violence with his description of Asians as "hideous and repulsive . . . a curse to our country, and a foul blot upon our civilization."[20]

The nineteenth century saw the end of slavery in the United States, and amendments to the Constitution gave former slaves the same rights held by White men. But Black Americans were not the only group to feel the sting of racial discrimination. Americans of Asian and Hispanic descent were also victims of racial prejudice and violence. These racist attitudes and actions did not end. Rather, they continued into the new century.

CHAPTER THREE

Racism in the Early Twentieth Century

Although the KKK's influence had ended by the turn of the twentieth century, White supremacists continued to terrorize Blacks. One of the most widespread means of intimidation was the act of lynching. According to a 2017 study by the Equal Justice Initiative, "Through lynching, Southern white communities asserted their racial dominance over the region's political and economic resources—a dominance first achieved through slavery would now be restored through blood and terror."[21]

In the American South lynching as a form of racial intimidation began in the 1830s. By the early 1900s lynch mobs had killed thousands of innocent Blacks. There were about twenty-five hundred lynchings from 1890 to 1910, with Blacks accounting for almost 80 percent of the victims. Whites who opposed racism by helping Blacks were often lynched as well. In what had become public exhibitions, lynchings were staged before crowds of hundreds or even thousands of spectators. Photographs of the victims' bodies were published in newspapers and made into postcards sold as souvenirs. These postcards often contained printed captions or intimidating messages. One showed a photograph of four Black lynching victims and a poem underneath that contained these lines:

The negro, now,
by eternal grace,
Must learn to stay in the negro's place.
In the Sunny South, the land of the Free,
Let the WHITE SUPREME forever be.[22]

One of the most horrific incidents of lynching occurred in 1916 in Waco, Texas. Seventeen-year-old Jesse Washington, a Black farmhand, was accused of killing his female employer. Washington admitted his guilt in a brief trial, but before court officials could escort him away, a mob dragged him from the courtroom. Washington was beaten, stabbed, hanged from a tree, mutilated, and burned to death in a fire in front of Waco's city hall. A crowd of ten thousand to fifteen thousand mostly White spectators, including children, witnessed the gruesome scene. No one did anything to stop the violence. Some onlookers cheered and collected souvenirs cut from Washington's body.

The gruesome death of Jesse Washington, though tragic, helped turn public opinion against such ugly spectacles. As photographs of the lynching circulated, public disgust began to grow. The recently founded National Association for the Advancement of Colored People (NAACP) saw new support for its justice campaign for Black Americans.

Rebirth of the KKK

As opinions on brutality against Blacks were beginning to change in the early twentieth century, the emerging medium of motion pictures began offering a new kind of entertainment. But sometimes those motion pictures touched on topics of public concern. Early movies were crude by modern standards, filmed in black and white with no sound, and most running just a few minutes in length. One of the earliest full-length motion pictures was 1915's *The Birth of a Nation*, a three-hour epic story of the Civil War and Reconstruction. Directed by cinema pioneer D.W. Griffith, the film became a national sensation but also helped inspire a new wave of racism in America.

The gruesome spectacle of lynchings became a favorite tool of racial intimidation—even into the early twentieth century. Lynch mobs killed thousands of innocent Blacks and some Whites too.

The Birth of a Nation, based on a novel entitled *The Clansman*, presented the Civil War and Reconstruction eras through a distorted lens of White supremacy. It depicted the antebellum South as a paradise for slaves, who happily toiled for their masters. In postwar scenes, however, newly freed Black men were depicted as ignorant, unruly thugs who lusted after White women and disrespected the White men that had once controlled their lives. The film ended with images of Klan members garbed in white robes setting crosses aflame. The clear message was that they were saving the South from the Black race.

The Birth of a Nation was a box-office hit. It also brought the KKK once more to the forefront of American racism. Inspired by the film, William J. Simmons, a Georgia minister, revived the original KKK, naming himself "Imperial Wizard." In November 1915 Simmons led his group of fifteen Klansmen to Stone Mountain near Atlanta. There they erected a burning cross to symbolize the rebirth

Desegregating the Military

The Japanese attack on Pearl Harbor in Hawaii brought the United States into World War II in 1941. At the time, only about four thousand Black Americans were serving in the armed forces. By the end of the war in 1945, that number had grown to more than 1 million African Americans in uniform.

Harry S. Truman succeeded President Franklin D. Roosevelt upon Roosevelt's death in 1945. As a senator in 1940, Truman had made his views on racism known. "I believe in the brotherhood of man," he stated, "not merely the brotherhood of white men but the brotherhood of all men before the law." In 1946 Truman created the President's Committee on Civil Rights to examine the status of prejudice in America. The committee reported that the US military had a poor record concerning the treatment of minorities in uniform and recommended that the armed forces be desegregated. On July 26, 1948, Truman issued Executive Order 9981, banning segregation in the armed services, and a new committee was formed to carry out Truman's order. Although the navy and air force readily complied, the army remained segregated until the Korean War of 1950 to 1953.

Quoted in David McCullough, *Truman*. Simon & Schuster, 1992, p. 247.

of the KKK. "Under a blazing, fiery torch," said Simmons, "the Invisible Empire was called from its slumber of half a century to take up a new task and fulfill a new mission for humanity's good."[23] That new mission was keeping White supremacy alive and powerful. By 1921 the KKK boasted nearly one hundred thousand members.

Although less violent than the original KKK, whippings, beatings, and lynchings still occurred. Blacks were not the only targets of the revived Klan: Jews, Catholics, and immigrants were added to the KKK's list of enemies. Instead of holding secret meetings, the new Klan embraced public displays that included huge parades, outdoor carnivals, and stirring speeches. Newspaper advertisements solicited new members, and many who would never think of joining nevertheless agreed with the Klan's racist philosophy.

> "Under a blazing, fiery torch the Invisible Empire [of the KKK] was called from its slumber of half a century to take up a new task and fulfill a new mission for humanity's good."[23]
>
> —KKK Imperial Wizard William J. Simmons

War and Racism

While enthusiasm for *The Birth of a Nation* swept the United States, across the Atlantic Europe was embroiled in a conflict known as the Great War, with France and its allies fighting against nations allied with Germany. When the United States entered the war in 1917, Blacks saw an opportunity to earn the respect of White America by joining the military. Some 380,000 Black Americans eventually served during the war. The US military at the time was segregated. The navy allowed Blacks to perform only unskilled tasks, and the marines barred them from joining altogether. Blacks could also serve in segregated units of the army. One especially honored Black regiment, the 369th Infantry, known as the Harlem Hellfighters, fought courageously on the battlefields of France.

When the war ended in 1918, American troops were hailed as heroes as they returned from Europe. Despite the bravery of Black soldiers during the war, however, homecoming for them

Members of the 369th Infantry Regiment, known as the Harlem Hellfighters, celebrate their return to the United States around 1919. Despite serving with distinction on the battlefields of France during World War I, respect at home was elusive.

> "Every loyal American negro who has served with the colors may fairly ask: 'Is this our reward for what we have done?'"[24]
>
> —*New York Evening Sun*

did not result in the new respect for which they had hoped. White Americans feared that Black soldiers would use their military training to forcibly achieve the equality they felt they deserved. Violence soon followed as White supremacists fought to keep Blacks in their place. One month after the war ended, Charles Lewis, an honorably discharged army veteran, was arrested for an alleged robbery. Taken to jail in his hometown in Kentucky, Lewis was dragged from his cell by a mob of one hundred angry Whites and lynched, still wearing his army uniform. In reporting the lynching, the *New York Evening Sun* concluded, "Every loyal American negro who has served with the colors may fairly ask: 'Is this our reward for what we have done?'"[24]

Red Summer

With the war over and thousands of Black veterans back home, racial tensions flared in the summer of 1919 as White mob brutality against Blacks spread. The violence was not limited to the southern states. Beginning in 1916 millions of Blacks had left the rural South and headed to cities in the North to escape segregation and search for work in northern factories. Called the Great Migration, this mass movement brought African Americans to New York, Chicago, Detroit, and other major industrial centers. Lured by higher wages (factory workers could earn three times what they had made on southern farms) and plentiful job openings, hope for a new life ran high in urban Black communities.

But while they had escaped the scourge of the Jim Crow South, Blacks migrating to the North soon encountered racism there as well. White individuals (including many recent immigrants) worked side by side with Black individuals in factories, railroads, and steel mills, but many of those White workers considered their Black coworkers inferior. Competition for jobs and housing added to the stressful atmosphere. Beginning in April

1919 these tensions boiled over in what became known as Red Summer. This was a series of violent confrontations in the South and the North. The earliest violent incident occurred on April 14 when six people, two White police officers and four Black men, were killed in a riot at a Black church in Jenkins County, Georgia.

One of the worst racial clashes of the summer began on July 27 in Chicago. On this hot Sunday, a seventeen-year-old Black youth named Eugene Williams was swimming in Lake Michigan. He inadvertently drifted into an area commonly understood as reserved for White swimmers. Along the beach White men began throwing rocks at Williams, one of which struck him, causing him to drown. Although witnesses pointed out the man responsible for the fatal throw, White police officers refused to arrest him, detaining a Black man instead. Outraged at this injustice, a crowd of Blacks clashed with White mobs, and soon the violence spread from the beach to South Side neighborhoods.

For the next seven days, Blacks and Whites battled each other with guns, knives, rocks, clubs, and any other weapons they could find. Houses were looted and burned, leaving nearly

Riot on Black Wall Street

The worst race riot in US history took place in Tulsa, Oklahoma, in the spring of 1921. Following the arrest of a Black teen accused of assault, a mob decided to take the law into their own hands. Assembling at the courthouse where the teen was being held, the mob failed in their efforts to seize him. A group of Blacks hoping to prevent a lynching soon arrived, and when a gunshot rang out, the two groups clashed, resulting in twelve deaths.

The next morning violence erupted in Tulsa's Greenwood neighborhood. Known as Black Wall Street, Greenwood was home to prosperous African Americans. Black Wall Street could have become a shining example of the possibilities open to African Americans. But the riot changed all that as armed confrontations broke out between Blacks and Whites. Black homes and businesses were looted and burned to the ground.

National Guardsmen were summoned to restore order, but instead they brought machine guns to intimidate the residents into submission. Blacks were herded at gunpoint into makeshift internment camps. When the riot finally ended, some three hundred people had been killed, and thirty-five city blocks were totally destroyed.

one thousand Black Chicagoans homeless. The riot ended when units of the Illinois state militia arrived to restore order. Chicago's Red Summer riot left thirty-eight dead (twenty-three Black and fifteen White individuals) and more than five hundred injured.

By November, Red Summer had run its course. Despite their losses, Black Americans had found new courage to fight back against racism. Through their actions, they also laid the groundwork for the movement that would eventually help them achieve their civil rights.

Confining the Japanese

While African Americans were building the foundation for reclaiming their civil rights, another minority group was about to be stripped of their rights as American citizens. The Japanese attack on Pearl Harbor in Hawaii on December 7, 1941, drew the United States into World War II. Citizens in the western states of California, Oregon, and Washington feared that many of the 120,000 Japanese Americans living on the West Coast could be covert spies or saboteurs. Newspaper columnist Henry McLemore, in a racially based tirade, proposed a solution to the "problem" of the Japanese in America. "I am for the immediate removal of every Japanese on the West Coast," he wrote, "to a point deep in the interior. I don't mean a nice part of the interior either. Herd 'em up, pack 'em off and give 'em the inside room in the badlands. . . . Personally, I hate the Japanese. And that goes for all of them."[25]

Public sentiment against the Japanese in the West grew. On February 19, 1942, President Franklin D. Roosevelt signed Executive Order 9066 authorizing the removal of all people of Japanese descent on the West Coast to camps in remote locations. The internees could take only what they could carry, leaving behind their homes, farms, and businesses. There were ten internment camps, called "relocation centers," spread throughout the West, some built in barren deserts that subjected the internees to harsh weather. Families lived in crowded barracks that lacked plumbing or kitchens. Work was sometimes available to relieve the monot-

In a photograph taken by famed photographer Dorothea Lange, worry and confusion show on the faces of two young Japanese Americans awaiting relocation with their families in 1942. By the time they were allowed to return home, many had lost everything.

ony of camp life. Children attended school in the camps, although there were few textbooks or adequate supplies.

The war ended in 1945, and by the next year all the internment camps were closed. Free to return home, many of the internees found their dwellings and businesses gone or in disrepair. Property stored for safekeeping had been vandalized or stolen, and farms were overgrown with weeds, their crops destroyed. Jobs were hard to find: businesses displayed signs in their windows proclaiming, "No Japs Wanted."[26] It took more than forty years—until 1988—for the US government to apologize and pay reparations of $20,000 to each living former internee—more than eighty-two thousand Japanese Americans.

Racism survived the turn of the century in the white-robed KKK, the riots that rocked many American cities, and the internment of innocent Japanese Americans. In the latter part of the century, however, a new movement promised to bring awareness of racism to the forefront of the American conscience.

CHAPTER FOUR

The Civil Rights Era

Every day, Linda Brown walked to a bus stop, where she waited for the school bus to take her to Monroe Elementary School in Topeka, Kansas. In all types of weather, Linda was forced to walk six blocks, crossing a busy street and a dangerous railroad switching yard, to reach a bus stop where she would wait for the bus to take her to her all-Black school. Another school, Sumner Elementary, was only four blocks from Linda's home. Oliver Brown, Linda's father, had tried to enroll her there, but his request was denied. Kansas in the 1950s adhered to the 1896 *Plessy v. Ferguson* Supreme Court decision upholding the legality of segregated public facilities. Linda could not attend Sumner because it was for Whites only, and she was Black.

The NAACP had long hoped to end this type of segregation. To achieve that goal, it filed lawsuits in four states (South Carolina, Virginia, Delaware, and Kansas) and the District of Columbia. The Kansas lawsuit was filed on behalf of the Brown family of Topeka. The lawsuits contended that the all-Black schools were inferior to the all-White schools. In all five cases the lower courts ruled against the families. In 1952 the Supreme Court agreed to hear the cases, which were combined under the name *Brown v. Board of Education*.

A Landmark Ruling on Segregated Schools

Beginning on December 9 of that year, the justices heard arguments in the case. Filling the courtroom were some three hundred spectators, both Black and White, eager to witness a history-making event. John Davis, a renowned attorney from South Carolina, argued on behalf of the school districts that the "separate but equal" issue had already been decided in the *Plessy* case and that the states were already working on making facilities equal. Thurgood Marshall, the attorney for the families, countered that teaching methods, textbooks, and school facilities for Black students were inferior to those provided for White students. A child psychologist named Kenneth Clark presented evidence of experiments indicating that attending segregated schools had a harmful effect on Black children. Marshall concluded that his opponents wanted the court to make "an inherent determination that the people who were formerly in slavery . . . shall be kept as near that stage as possible."[27]

After an extended period of deliberation, Chief Justice Earl Warren announced the court's unanimous decision on May 17, 1954:

> To separate [Black children] from others of similar age and qualifications solely because of their race generates a feeling of inferiority as to their status in the community that may affect their hearts and minds in a way unlikely ever to be undone. . . . We conclude that in the field of public education the doctrine of "separate but equal" has no place. Separate educational facilities are inherently unequal.[28]

With this decision, legal segregation in America's public schools was struck down. But controversy over the decision would grow.

Opposition to the *Brown* ruling was intense in the South. One of the most ardent opponents of desegregation was Senator Harry Byrd of Virginia. In 1956 Byrd and one hundred other southern senators and representatives signed a statement known as the Southern Manifesto, which claimed that the Supreme Court had overstepped its legal authority with the *Brown* decision. In the fall of 1956, boards of education across the South delayed opening their schools in order to avoid integrating them; many schools closed permanently. In many areas, White parents established private schools so that their children would not have to attend public schools with Black students. Known as segregation academies, these schools were financed in part by tax dollars, which reduced funds available for public schools attended by Black students.

Racial tensions intensified as laws forcing southern schools to integrate fueled clashes between Blacks and Whites, both students and parents. In the state capital of Arkansas, such tensions prompted the president of the United States to call out the military to achieve the goal of desegregation.

Racism in Little Rock

In September 1957 nine Black students were prepared to begin fall classes at Central High School in Little Rock, Arkansas, the first to attend the school under the *Brown* desegregation ruling. They were met by a crowd of almost one thousand protesters, who shouted racial epithets and insults at the students. Fearing that violence would erupt, school administrators sent the nine students home at midday.

The mayor of Little Rock asked President Dwight Eisenhower for federal help to prevent violence, and on September 25 the students, now known as the Little Rock Nine, were escorted to class by soldiers of the US Army's 101st Airborne Division. Although they could now attend classes, the nine students suffered verbal and often physical abuse from White classmates. Every day for weeks the Little Rock Nine had to pass through crowds of jeering protesters to enter Central High. "It was like going into battle every day,"[29] Ernest Green later recalled. Green, who was a senior at

> "It was like going into battle every day."[29]
>
> —Little Rock Nine student Ernest Green

Eight of the nine Black students attending Little Rock's Central High in October 1957 walk from school to a waiting army vehicle. The Little Rock Nine, as they came to be known, stood their ground despite extreme resistance and threats of violence.

the time, became the first African American to graduate from Central. Green and the others all went on to obtain college educations. It took until 1972 for all the schools in Little Rock to be fully desegregated.

Violence Against Hispanics

In the decades before the Supreme Court ruling on segregated schools, racial insults and violence had spilled over into other areas of American life. In the 1930s and 1940s, large numbers of people from Mexico were immigrating to the United States. In many places, Hispanics were barred from public facilities or restricted to segregated areas. Anti-Hispanic racism also included incidents of mob violence, illegal deportations, and lynchings. As the United States suffered from the Great Depression in the 1930s, a series of mass deportations sent nearly 2 million people of Mexican descent, many of them US citizens, across the southern border to Mexico. Referred to by the innocent-sounding term *repatriation drives*, the deportations were usually carried out by local police, who staged raids in places where Hispanics gathered. In one incident in February 1931, armed police officers and immigration officials raided a Mexican open-air market plaza on Olvera Street in Los Angeles. The officers sealed off the plaza and rounded up about four hundred Hispanic people, ordering them to show proof of their citizenship. (While some countries require citizens to carry such documents with them at all times, the United States has never done so.) Those who could not provide papers were detained and ultimately sent by train to Mexico.

Other workers were deported by employers who feared getting into trouble with immigration officials. Some of these employers drove their Hispanic employees to the border and dropped them off in Mexico. Others paid airfare for Hispanic workers to leave the country. Even hospital patients, including those with serious conditions such as tuberculosis or mental illness, were removed from hospitals and taken across the border. Many families were separated by the deportations.

The Kerner Commission

More than one hundred race riots broke out in major US cities during the summer of 1967. These riots resulted in the deaths of nearly seventy people in Detroit, Michigan, and Newark, New Jersey, as well as casualties in many other cities. President Lyndon Johnson established a commission to investigate the causes of the rioting.

Illinois governor Otto Kerner was appointed to head the commission, which would bear his name. The eleven commission members spent six months visiting inner-city neighborhoods and gathering facts. In March 1968 the Kerner Commission published its findings. It was an indictment of the disparity between White and Black economic and social structures: "Our nation is moving toward two societies, one Black, one White—separate and unequal. White racism is essentially responsible for the explosive mixture which has been accumulating in our cities."

The commission debated the use of the word *racism* before agreeing to include it. Said one commissioner, "Our saying racism, I think, was very important to a lot of black people who said, 'Well, maybe it's not just me. Maybe I'm not, by myself, at fault here. Maybe there's something else going on.'"

Quoted in Jess Engebretson and Matthew Green, "The Summer of Rage: Lessons from the Race Riots in Detroit and Newark 50 Years Ago," KQED, July 24, 2017. www.kqed.org.

In 1943 a White mob in Los Angeles attacked young Hispanic men wearing clothing known as zoot suits. Instead of arresting the perpetrators, police arrested the young men. They are shown here awaiting a bus ride to court.

By 1936 the deportations had ended, but as World War II cast its shadow over the world, Hispanics still felt the sting of racism. In 1943 Whites and Hispanics in Los Angeles clashed, not over language barriers or religious practices but the wearing of a particular type of garment called a zoot suit. Popular with Hispanic teens, zoot suits featured long jackets with large lapels and padded shoulders, along with wide, loose-fitting pants. Many Whites felt that the suits, with their excessive amounts of fabric, were wasteful and unpatriotic during wartime rationing of food, gasoline, and other essentials. To others, teens who wore zoot suits were simply hoodlums and troublemakers.

In June 1943 Hispanics and others wearing zoot suits were attacked and stripped of their controversial garments. According to a witness, "Marching through the streets of downtown Los Angeles, a mob of several thousand soldiers, sailors, and civilians, proceeded to beat up every zoot suiter they could find. . . . Streetcars were halted while Mexicans, and some Filipinos and

Negroes, were jerked from their seats, pushed into the streets and beaten with a sadistic frenzy."[30]

During several days of chaos, the police did nothing to stop the White rioters but instead arrested some five hundred Hispanics. The rioters, military and civilian, were praised in the press for helping suppress what they characterized as a Mexican crime wave. The victims of the zoot suit riots were attacked simply for expressing their fashion preference and being different from the White majority.

> "Streetcars were halted while Mexicans, and some Filipinos and Negroes, were jerked from their seats, pushed into the streets and beaten with a sadistic frenzy."[30]
>
> —Witness to zoot suit riots

Freedom Riders

Hostility between the races continued to surface even into the 1960s. Against this backdrop, bold challenges to the status quo also continued. During this decade, long-distance bus travel was a common mode of transportation in the United States. In the South the buses and their support facilities remained segregated: signs denoting "White" and "Colored" waiting rooms and rest-rooms were prominently displayed. In 1960, however, the Supreme Court ruled that that all buses and bus stations operating on interstate routes must be integrated. In May 1961 a racially mixed group of mostly college students called Freedom Riders boarded buses that would take them through several southern states to test compliance with the court's decision.

What began as a social experiment soon turned into a nightmare of racial hatred and bloody violence. In Alabama, Georgia, and Mississippi, the Freedom Riders were met by violent mobs of White supremacists. In Birmingham, Alabama, a bus was forced off the road and set on fire. When another bus stopped at Montgomery, Alabama, a mob of Whites attacked the Freedom Riders with baseball bats, bottles, and iron pipes. Local police did not intervene. Although many riders suffered severe injuries, segregation laws prohibited ambulances from taking Blacks to the hospital, and White cab drivers refused to transport both Black and White victims.

In all, more than sixty freedom rides took place. Many of these rides, and the young people who took part in them, were featured on television news and in newspaper stories nationwide. Their actions won public support. In November 1961 the Interstate Commerce Commission officially prohibited segregation in interstate travel.

Triumph and Tragedy

The civil rights movement of the 1960s saw both triumph and tragedy. Early in the decade Baptist minister and civil rights activist Dr. Martin Luther King Jr. had become a voice of reason amid the racial violence. His message of nonviolent protest reached its high point in the March on Washington in August 1963. Some 250,000 people of all ages and races gathered at the Lincoln Memorial for a day of inspirational songs and uplifting words from numerous speakers, culminating in King's iconic "I Have a Dream"

Mexican Laborers

World War II resulted in a shortage of American workers. To make up for this shortage, in 1942 the US government created the Bracero program. Under this program, Mexican laborers (braceros) were allowed to temporarily work in the United States. The program could not provide enough laborers, however, so illegal immigration helped satisfy the need. But by the 1950s Americans were becoming upset with the great number of Mexicans crossing the border. In 1954 President Dwight Eisenhower devised a plan to send unauthorized immigrants back to Mexico.

The mission of Operation Wetback (named for a derogatory term given to unauthorized Mexican immigrants) was to organize a mass deportation. Using military-style tactics, the US Border Patrol rounded up Mexicans—including some US citizens—in Texas, California, and elsewhere. US Border Patrol agents put the immigrants on trains, trucks, and planes headed for Mexico.

US officials touted the operation as a success. Historian Kelly Lytle Hernandez describes it differently. Operation Wetback, she says, "was lawless; it was arbitrary; it was based on a lot of xenophobia, and it resulted in sizable large-scale violations of people's rights, including the forced deportation of U.S. citizens."

Quoted in Erin Blakemore, "The Largest Mass Deportation in American History," History, June 18, 2019. www .history.com.

speech. The event helped raise awareness of racial inequality, but the peaceful theme could not prevent further violence between Blacks and Whites.

Freedom Summer, a 1964 campaign to register Black voters in Mississippi, created an immediate racist backlash. White Mississippians resented the out-of-state volunteers and their interference in local affairs. White mobs beat volunteer campaign workers and had many others arrested. Numerous Black churches were burned to the ground. Members of the KKK (including a local deputy sheriff) brutally murdered three volunteers, James Chaney, Andrew Goodman, and Michael Schwerner. Their bodies remained buried under an earthen dam until officials discovered them following a six-week search.

Marches protesting racial inequality increased as the 1960s wore on. On March 7, 1965, some six hundred protesters began a peaceful march in Selma, Alabama, in support of their constitutional right to vote. While attempting to cross a bridge to reach their destination of Montgomery, Alabama, the marchers were set upon by state troopers, who blocked their advance, beat them, and used tear gas to disperse the crowd. The violent incident became known as Bloody Sunday.

One hundred years after the end of the Civil War, racism was still embedded in American life. But times were changing, and the 1960s became the decade in which that change gained momentum. Social essayist Bruce Bawer describes the decade's impact on American society:

> The period was a desperately needed corrective that drew attention to America's injustices and started us down the road toward greater fairness and equality for all. . . . There was a general understanding and acceptance, as there had not been in the 1950s, that integration was America's future. . . . Most Americans of goodwill seemed to have accepted the idea that they were witnessing, if not taking an active role in, a process of social change that was essentially positive and that would in time bring greater social harmony.[31]

CHAPTER FIVE

A New Century and an Old Problem

Anh "Peng" Taylor, a ninety-four-year-old woman of Chinese and Vietnamese descent, was taking a walk in her San Francisco neighborhood in June 2021 when a stranger approached her. Without warning he stabbed her several times, running away and leaving her bleeding from numerous wounds. Taylor was rushed to the hospital, where she was treated for her injuries. From her hospital bed, a recovering Taylor asked, "Why would something like this happen to me?"[32]

The answer to that question illustrates a growing problem in America: anti-Asian racism. The attack on Taylor came just a month after another unprovoked attack in San Francisco injured two Asian American women at a bus stop. Race-based crimes against Americans of Asian descent are on the rise in the twenty-first century. A coalition called Stop AAPI Hate tracks incidents of violence and discrimination against Asian Americans and Pacific Islanders nationwide. From March 2020 to June 2021 it collected 9,081 reports of hate incidents against Asian Americans. Such incidents include verbal harassment and racial slurs, physical assault, discrimination in the workplace, vandalism, and online intimidation. Since the coronavirus that caused the COVID-19 pandemic originated in China, many Asian Americans have been subjected to racist comments such as "Go back where you came from," "You deserve to die," and "Kung Flu." But the recent increase in such racist behavior goes beyond hate incidents aimed at Asian Americans. People who have studied racism contend that it is a deeply rooted problem that continues to create barriers to equality.

Racism in Society

The deep roots of racism can be seen in many of the public institutions that are necessary for the smooth functioning of modern American society. Education, the criminal justice system, health care, and the government itself should operate for the good of all Americans. But according to many scholars and social researchers, hidden beneath the surface of these social necessities is a structure in which White people enjoy an advantage over people of color. This is called systemic (also called structural or institutional) racism, and it is widespread. "Systemic racism is so embedded in our societal interactions," says Boston science teacher Jo Persad, "that racism has become normalized and rendered nearly invisible."[33]

Evidence of systemic racism can be found in nearly every aspect of daily life. In America's educational system, Black students are more likely to attend schools that have less funding and poorer resources than schools with mostly White students. Black students are more likely to be referred to law enforcement for infractions of school rules and are three times more likely to be suspended. In addition, police sometimes use physical force on Black students. In a Chicago high school in 2019, a Black sixteen-year-old girl who had disobeyed a teacher was dragged down a flight of stairs and stunned by a Taser three times by two Chicago police officers. A cell phone video of the confrontation prompted national outrage.

Black Americans experience prejudice in other areas of life as well. In housing, prospective home buyers who are Black are shown fewer housing choices than White prospects and are often steered toward homes in poorer neighborhoods. Health care for Black patients is often of lower quality than

> "Systemic racism is so embedded in our societal interactions that racism has become normalized and rendered nearly invisible."[33]
>
> —Teacher Jo Persad

A Stop Asian Hate rally and march take place in April 2021 in Troy, Michigan. Racist attacks—verbal, physical, and online—against Asian Americans have increased nationwide since the start of the coronavirus pandemic in 2020.

for White patients, leading to less effective care and higher mortality. According to National Academy of Medicine, Blacks suffering from serious heart conditions are less likely to receive the most effective treatments, such as coronary bypass operations, and are discharged from the hospital earlier than White patients. Black Americans undergo more amputations, have less access to emergency services, and exhibit a lower average life expectancy than White Americans.

Racism and the Law

Another area that experiences the impact of institutional racism is the American criminal justice system. Judicial racism has its roots in history, says Radley Balko, author and civil rights journalist for the *Washington Post*:

> We have systems and institutions that produce racially disparate outcomes, regardless of the intentions of the people who work within them. When you consider that much of the criminal justice system was built, honed and

firmly established during the Jim Crow era—an era almost everyone, conservatives included, will concede [was] rife with racism—this is pretty intuitive. The modern criminal justice system helped preserve racial order—it kept black people in their place. For much of the early 20th century, in some parts of the country, that was its primary function. That it might retain some of those proclivities today shouldn't be all that surprising.[34]

The Sentencing Project, an initiative that promotes reforms in sentencing and incarceration policies, notes that there is a double standard in the criminal justice system, one for wealthy Whites and another for poor Blacks. Blacks are arrested and convicted more often than Whites and are consistently given harsher sentences. Although they are only about 13 percent of the US population, Blacks made up some 34 percent of the prison population in 2018. Racial bias also exists in the courtroom: Blacks are more likely to be dismissed from jury selection for a variety of reasons, including physical appearance, the assumption of lower intelligence, and other reasons based on race. According to a report from the Equal Justice Initiative, "Some district attorney's offices explicitly train prosecutors to exclude racial minorities from jury service and teach them how to mask racial bias to avoid a finding that antidiscrimination laws have been violated."[35]

> "The modern criminal justice system helped preserve racial order—it kept black people in their place."[34]
>
> —Journalist Radley Balko

Blacks and Law Enforcement

Along with jury duty, most people experience their only encounter with the justice system while behind the wheel. For White motorists, being pulled over by police can be an unnerving but usually nonthreatening incident. For Black drivers, however, an encoun-

Critical Race Theory

Critical race theory (CRT) is an academic study developed in the 1970s by legal scholars to explore how racism is embedded in America's social institutions. CRT initially focused on racism in the US legal system, but it expanded to explore how schools represent minorities in the teaching of US history. While students learn about the achievements of White people, the brutal truth of sacrifices suffered by indigenous people, Blacks, and other minorities who were pushed aside, enslaved, and killed in the name of progress receive less attention.

The concepts of CRT are generally too advanced for K–12 schools, and there is no evidence that it is being taught in those schools. Nevertheless, it has sparked controversy. Teachers in many school districts across the country have been threatened and may face fines or lose their jobs if they teach CRT—or, in some cases, almost anything to do with racial bias. Numerous parent groups and some state and local legislative bodies have loudly opposed CRT, arguing that it attempts to rewrite American history and instill guilt in White students. As of August 2021, eight states had passed legislation that bans teaching the principles of CRT; at least fifteen more were planning to introduce similar legislation.

---

ter with law enforcement can become deadly. Thirty-two-year-old Philando Castile was a victim of a fatal traffic stop in 2016 in a suburb of Saint Paul, Minnesota. Castile was pulled over because the officers thought he looked like a wanted robbery suspect. Castile immediately informed them, as was proper, that he had a licensed gun in his car. He then began to retrieve his identification from the glove compartment. Fearing Castile was reaching for the weapon, an officer shot seven times, killing Castile as he sat in his car.

A 2020 study published in the journal *Nature Human Behaviour* studied nearly 100 million traffic stops nationwide. Researchers discovered that Black drivers were 20 percent more likely to be pulled over by police than White drivers. The study noted a fact that demonstrates how race plays a part in African American traffic stops. Black drivers were less likely to be pulled over late in the day or at night, when darkness can make it more difficult for the police to determine whether a driver is Black or White.

Once a traffic stop is made, Black drivers are more often subjected to searches, even though statistics show that White drivers are more likely to be caught with contraband such as drugs or drug paraphernalia in their vehicles. Blacks are also twice as likely not to be told the reason for a traffic stop. The frequency of these types of interactions on the road has turned the phrase "driving while Black" into a common and disturbing refrain.

Black Lives Matter

Relations between Black Americans and police fell to new lows on May 25, 2020. On that date, a forty-six-year-old Black man named George Floyd was arrested in Minneapolis, Minnesota, on suspicion of passing a counterfeit twenty-dollar bill. Derek Chauvin, one of the responding police officers, subdued Floyd by kneeling on his neck long enough to cause Floyd's death by asphyxiation. After a six-week trial in 2021, Chauvin (who is White) was found guilty of murder and sentenced to twenty-two and a half years in prison.

Public outcry over the killing of George Floyd began almost immediately after the incident. "I can't breathe," words repeatedly uttered by Floyd as he lay pinned on the ground, became a rallying cry for protesters across the nation. Among those leading the

The Black Lives Matter movement has focused attention on racial discrimination in policing and other areas of American life. Marchers make their views known during a 2020 demonstration in Teaneck, New Jersey.

protests was Black Lives Matter (BLM), an organization formed to raise awareness of racism embedded in the institutions of American society. BLM was founded in 2013 in response to the killing in Florida of Trayvon Martin, an unarmed Black teenager, by a neighborhood watch co-ordinator. Alicia Garza, an activist living in Oakland, California, and two other activists, Patrisse Cullors and Opal Tometi, formed a grassroots organization to respond to growing racist violence against Blacks. They used the hashtag #BlackLivesMatter. It was, says Garza, "a call to action, to make sure we are creating a world where black lives actually do matter."[36] From this small beginning, BLM grew into an international movement, responding to the killing of Black Americans with protests and seeking justice for the victims.

> "[BLM is] a call to action, to make sure we are creating a world where black lives actually do matter."[36]
>
> —BLM cofounder Alicia Garza

Racist backlash to BLM was swift. Although BLM protesters were generally peaceful, they were often blamed for the violent actions of non-BLM protesters who destroyed property and looted businesses. Disinformation on social media portrayed BLM as a violent, racist movement. The organization's phrase "Black Lives Matter" was countered by Whites who promoted the slogans "All Lives Matter" and "Blue Lives Matter," the latter in support of police. When New York City decided to paint "Black Lives Matter" in large letters on Fifth Avenue in July 2020, President Donald Trump called the phrase a "symbol of hate."[37]

In the three months after Floyd's death, more than 7,750 BLM demonstrations were staged by local organizers across the United States. As news reports of these protests hit the global media, the organization's influence became international. Protests against police violence after the Floyd killing were held in sixty-one nations around the world. In 2021 Black Lives Matter was nominated for a Nobel Peace Prize. The nomination described BLM as "the strongest global force against racial injustice."[38]

White Supremacy Evolves

In contrast to BLM, a growing array of White supremacist groups have made fear and violence an integral part of their campaign of racism. "White supremacists believe the white race is in danger of extinction—they feel like they are being replaced—and blame non-white people for their national economic troubles,"[39] say journalists Emanuela Campanella and Elizabeth Palmieri of Canada's Global News. The targets of these groups include not only African Americans but also Jews and Americans of Hispanic, Asian, and Middle Eastern descent.

Unlike the KKK and other groups that emerged during Reconstruction, today's White supremacist groups can spread their messages of hate quickly and easily through social media and other online platforms. "There certainly were hate groups before the Internet and social media," says political scientist Richard Hasen of the University of California, Irvine. Social media, he notes, makes it "easier to organize, to spread the word, for people to know where to go. . . . Social media has lowered the collective-action problems that individuals who might want to be in a hate group would face."[40]

Hate groups are often a troublesome presence at peaceful civil rights rallies. The Proud Boys, a group that formed in 2016, often deny a racist agenda but have shown up to disrupt minority rights rallies and school board meetings and have destroyed BLM property. The Southern Poverty Law Center, a legal advocacy organization that monitors hate group and White supremacist activities, has classified the Proud Boys as a hate group. Another, more loosely organized group known as the Boogaloo movement is an affiliation of men who hold a broad spectrum of beliefs. Many of the movement's followers share the views of White supremacists.

Today's White supremacists no longer look like the hooded riders of the nineteenth and early twentieth centuries. "They're not wearing the white robes of the [Ku Klux] Klan," says Barbara Perry, director of the Centre on Hate, Bias and Extremism at On-

The 1619 Project

In 2019 the *New York Times*, one of America's most respected newspapers, embarked on a project "to reframe the country's history by placing the consequences of slavery and the contributions of black Americans at the very center of our national narrative," explains Jake Silverstein, editor in chief of the *New York Times Magazine*. The project is named for the year that the first enslaved Blacks were brought to what would ultimately become the United States. The 1619 Project published a number of articles, poetry, and photographs to illustrate the impact of Blacks on American history.

Almost immediately, the 1619 Project became a lightning rod for controversy, especially in the area of education. The project developed a curriculum for teaching elementary and high school students about the role of Black people in US history. Critics say that it distorts American history and is racially divisive. In contrast, supporters believe it corrects the long-standing omission of the lasting impact Black Americans had, and continue to have, on society. Many conservative legislators have proposed laws forbidding schools from including it in their classrooms.

Jake Silverstein, "Why We Published the 1619 Project," *New York Times Magazine*, December 20, 2019. www.nytimes.com.

---

tario Tech University in Canada. "Many of them are white-collar workers. They're well educated, they're sophisticated in their use of technology, they're sophisticated in their language and their construction of narratives, so the movement really has changed its face."[41] But the White supremacists are recognizable nonetheless. At rallies and marches, some wear tactical protective gear and tote weapons, while others don Hawaiian shirts and military fatigues. Confederate battle flags and racist slogans are plentiful at these events.

Changing Attitudes Toward Racism

Although White supremacists are vocal, they actually represent a small segment of American society. What the majority of people think about racism and its impact on the nation can be obtained from public opinion polls. A 2020 poll cosponsored by NBC News and the *Wall Street Journal* revealed that voters today are more likely to acknowledge the reality of racial discrimination than they

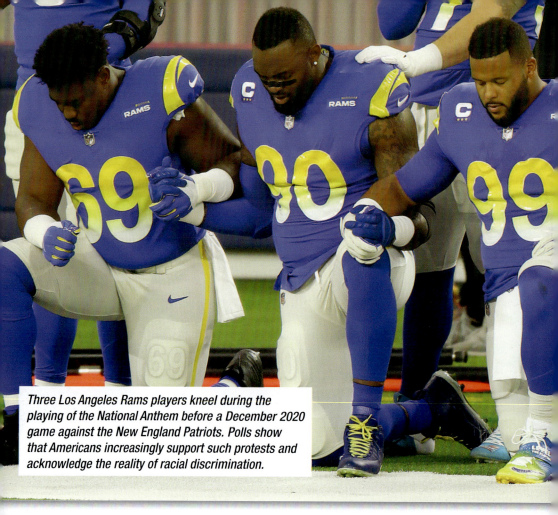

Three Los Angeles Rams players kneel during the playing of the National Anthem before a December 2020 game against the New England Patriots. Polls show that Americans increasingly support such protests and acknowledge the reality of racial discrimination.

were just over a decade ago. This applies to perceptions about bias against Black Americans, Hispanic Americans, and Asian Americans. In the same poll, more than half of US voters stated their support for protests against racism, including athletes kneeling in protest and the removal of Confederate-themed statues.

The poll also found that more than half of voters—56 percent—think that American society is racist. To be sure, the United States is not perfect; no nation is. The racism that underlies so many of the nation's social institutions is perhaps the most insidious of all of America's problems and the most difficult to root out. But, however slowly, progress is being made, and the momentum must be maintained by those who have the courage to identify America's weaknesses and turn them into strengths.

SOURCE NOTES

Introduction: The Idea of Race

1. Angela Onwuachi-Willig, "Race and Racial Identity Are Social Constructs," *New York Times*, September 6, 2016. www.nytimes.com.
2. Onwuachi-Willig, "Race and Racial Identity Are Social Constructs."
3. Quoted in Joshua Bote, "'Get in Good Trouble, Necessary Trouble': Rep. John Lewis in His Own Words," *USA Today*, July 19, 2020. www.usatoday.com.

Chapter One: Race and America's Beginnings

4. Declaration of Independence, National Archives, 2020. www.archives.gov.
5. Quoted in Charles W. Mills, *Black Rights/White Wrongs: The Critique of Racial Liberalism*. New York: Oxford, 2017, p. 173.
6. David Hume, "Essay XXI: Of Natural Characters," Hume Texts Online. www.davidhume.org.
7. US Constitution, National Archives, 2020. www.archives.gov.
8. Quoted in DeNeen L. Brown, "'Barbaric': America's Cruel History of Separating Children from Their Parents," *Washington Post*, May 31, 2018. www.washingtonpost.com.
9. Thomas Paine, *Common Sense*, Project Gutenberg, June 14, 2017. www.gutenberg.org.
10. Quoted in Anne C. Bailey, "They Sold Human Beings Here," 1619 Project, *New York Times Magazine*. www.nytimes.com.
11. Quoted in Larry Slawson, "The Impact of Nat Turner's Rebellion," Owlcation, June 30, 2021. www.owlcation.com.
12. "Dred Scott, Plaintiff in Error, v. John F.A. Sandford," Legal Information Institute. www.law.cornell.edu.

Chapter Two: Emancipation and Reconstruction

13. Abraham Lincoln, "First Inaugural Address," Avalon Project. www.avalon.law.yale.edu.
14. Quoted in Susan Campbell Bartoletti, *They Called Themselves the K.K.K.: The Birth of an American Terrorist Group*. New York: Houghton Mifflin, 2010, p. 8.

15. Abraham Lincoln, "Second Inaugural Address," Avalon Project. www.avalon.law.yale.edu.
16. Quoted in Michael Trinkley, "Free at Last, but Not for Long," South Carolina Information Highway. www.skiway.net.
17. US Constitution, National Archives, 2020. www.archives.gov.
18. Quoted in *American Experience*, "Jim Crow Laws," PBS. www.pbs.org.
19. Yuning Wu et al., "Race, Immigration, and Policing: Chinese Immigrants' Satisfaction with Police," *Justice Quarterly*, October 2011, p. 748.
20. Quoted in Kevin Waite, "The Bloody History of Anti-Asian Violence in the West," *National Geographic*, May 10, 2021. www.nationalgeographic.com.

Chapter Three: Racism in the Early Twentieth Century

21. Staff of the Equal Justice Initiative, *Lynching in America: Confronting the Legacy of Racial Terror*. Montgomery, AL: Equal Justice Initiative, 2017. https://eij.org.
22. Quoted in Patricia Bernstein, *The First Waco Horror: The Lynching of Jesse Washington and the Rise of the NAACP*. College Station: Texas A&M University Press, 2005, p. 54.
23. Quoted in Dick Lehr, *The Birth of a Nation: How a Legendary Filmmaker and a Crusading Editor Reignited America's Civil War*. New York: PublicAffairs, 2014, p. 278.
24. Quoted in Chad Williams, "African-American Veterans Hoped Their Service in World War I Would Secure Their Rights at Home. It Didn't," *Time*, November 12, 2018. www.time.com.
25. Henry McLemore, "This Is War! Stop Worrying About Hurting Jap Feelings," *Seattle Times*, January 30, 1942. www.densho.org.
26. Quoted in Jeffery F. Burton, et al., *"Confinement and Ethnicity: An Overview of World War II Japanese American Relocation Sites,"* National Park Service. www.nps.gov.

Chapter Four: The Civil Rights Era

27. Quoted in *Time*, "The Supreme Court: The Fading Line," December 21, 1953. www.time.com.
28. Earl Warren, *Brown v. The Board of Education of Topeka*, Landmark Cases. http://landmarkcases.c-span.org.
29. Quoted in Andrea Stone, "In Little Rock, a Small Act of Defiance Endures," *USA Today*, August 29, 2007. www.usatoday30.usatoday.com.

30. Quoted in Carey McWilliams, *North from Mexico: The Spanish-Speaking People of the United States*. Santa Barbara, CA: Praeger, 1990, p. 199.
31. Bruce Bawer, "The Other Sixties," *Wilson Quarterly*, Spring 2004. http://archive.wilsonquarterly.com.

Chapter Five: A New Century and an Old Problem

32. Quoted in Betty Yu, "Why Would Something Like This Happen to Me?' 94-Year-Old Anh 'Peng' Taylor Recovering After Shocking SF Stabbing Attack," KPIX, June 17, 2021. https://sanfrancisco.cbs local.com.
33. Quoted in Kate Slater, "What Is Systemic Racism?," *Today*, February 4, 2021. www.today.com.
34. Radley Balko, "There's Overwhelming Evidence That the Criminal Justice System Is Racist. Here's the Proof," *Washington Post*, June 10, 2020. www.washingtonpost.com.
35. Quoted in Equal Justice Initiative, "Illegal Racial Discrimination in Jury Selection: A Continuing Legacy," 2010. www.eji.org.
36. Quoted in Elizabeth Day, "#BlackLivesMatter: The Birth of a New Civil Rights Movement," *The Guardian* (Manchester, UK), July 19, 2015. www.the guardian.com.
37. Quoted in Max Cohen, "Trump: Black Lives Matter Is a 'Symbol of Hate.'" Politico, July 1, 2020. www.politico.com.
38. Quoted in Martin Belam, "Black Lives Matter Movement Nominated for Nobel Peace Prize," *The Guardian* (Manchester, UK), January 29, 2021. www.the guardian.com.
39. Emanuela Campanella and Elizabeth Palmieri, "The Rise of White Supremacy and Its New Face in the 21st Century," Global News, June 13, 2019. www.globalnews.ca.
40. Quoted in Francie Diep, "How Social Media Helped Organize and Radicalize America's White Supremacists," *Pacific Standard*, August 15, 2017. www.psmag.com.
41. Campanella and Palmieri, "The Rise of White Supremacy and Its New Face in the 21st Century."

ORGANIZATIONS AND WEBSITES

American Civil Liberties Union (ACLU)
www.aclu.org
The ACLU works to preserve the constitutional rights of all Americans through lobbying and litigation. Its website includes information on Supreme Court cases, an Action Center for local activism, and multimedia presentations about the ACLU's areas of concern.

History of Race in America, *Smithsonian*
www.smithsonianmag.com
This website is a compendium of resources on the history of American racism. It includes links to articles, videos, podcasts, and other resources that illuminate the problem of racial bias, from the earliest slaves to athletes taking a knee in protest.

Lynching in America: Confronting the Legacy of Racial Terror, Equal Justice Initiative
https://lynchinginamerica.eji.org
This report covers the history of lynching from its earliest incidents to its legacy, which has had a powerful effect on Blacks and Whites alike. It includes historical illustrations and photographs, lynching statistics by state, and graphic and disturbing descriptions of the horror of lynching.

National Association for the Advancement of Colored People (NAACP)
www.naacp.org
The NAACP fights against race-based discrimination in all areas of society: education, policing, housing, and business. With 2 million members, the organization supports grassroots activism for social justice. The NAACP website offers a resource library and current news about civil rights.

Segregation in America, Equal Justice Initiative
https://segregationinamerica.eji.org
This website explores the spread of racial bigotry in the United States. It includes information on activities of the civil rights era, profiles of segregationists, and information on the iconography of White supremacy. Videos document the civil rights era.

1619 Project, *New York Times Magazine*
www.nytimes.com
This controversial project strives to illustrate the impact of racism on all of American history. The website includes articles, essays, poetry, a visual history of slavery, and a school curriculum.

Southern Poverty Law Center (SPLC)
www.splcenter.org
The SPLC sponsors legal action in all areas of civil rights. It litigates for the rights of children, immigrants, LGBTQ individuals, and voters. Its *Hatewatch* blog examines the activity of the radical right, and an interactive map monitors the growth of hate groups.

FOR FURTHER RESEARCH

Books

Michael Eric Dyson, *Long Time Coming: Reckoning with Race in America*. New York: St. Martin's, 2020.

Patrisse Khan-Cullors and asha bandele, *When They Call You a Terrorist: A Story of Black Lives Matter and the Power to Change the World*. New York: Wednesday, 2020.

Kenrya Rankin, *Words of Change: Anti-racism: Powerful Voices, Inspiring Ideas*. Seattle, WA: Spruce, 2020.

Jason Reynolds and Ibram X. Kendi, *Stamped (for Kids): Racism, Antiracism, and You*. New York: Little, Brown, 2021.

Rachel Marie-Crane Williams, *Elegy for Mary Turner: An Illustrated Account of a Lynching*. New York: Verso, 2021.

Internet Sources

Erin Blakemore, "A Century of Trauma at U.S. Boarding Schools for Native American Children," *National Geographic*, July 9, 2021. www.nationalgeographic.com.

Shannon Luibrand, "How a Death in Ferguson Sparked a Movement in America," CBS News, August 7, 2015. www.cbsnews.com.

Erik Ortiz, "Inside 100 Million Police Traffic Stops: New Evidence of Racial Bias," NBC News, March 13, 2019. www.nbcnews.com.

INDEX

Note: Boldface page numbers indicate illustrations.

abolitionists and abolition, 20, 24
Anti-Coolie Act (California, 1862), 28
armed forces, Blacks in, 32, **33**
Arthur, Chester A., 26
Asians and Pacific Islanders
    Chinese immigrants, 7, 26–28
    Japanese Americans and Japanese immigrants, 8, 36–37, **37**
    Stop Asian Hate rally, **49**
    violent attacks against (2021), 47
Atlantic (magazine), 15
Atlantic slave trade, 7, **8**, 11–12

Balko, Radley, 49–50
Bawer, Bruce, 46
Bibb, Henry, 12–13
Birmingham, Alabama, and Freedom Riders, 44
The Birth of a Nation (movie), 30–31
Black codes (laws), 23
Black Lives Matter (BLM), **52**, 53, 54
Blacks
    in armed forces, 32, **33**
    Atlantic slave trade, 7, **8**, 11–12
    Great Migration, 34
    Jim Crow laws, 7, 25–27, 49–50
    lynchings of, 29–30, **31**, 34
    riots (1967), 41
    systemic racism and, 48–52
    See also segregation
Black Wall Street (Tulsa's Greenwood neighborhood), 35
Bloody Sunday, 46
Booth, John Wilkes, 21
Bracero program, 45
Brown, Linda, 38
Brown, Oliver, 38
Brown v. Board of Education (1954), 38–39
Byrd, Harry, 39–40

California
    Chinese in, 28
    Hispanics in
        arrests and beatings of, for wearing zoot suits, **43**, 43–44
        Greaser Law (1855), 16

Campanella, Emanuela, 54
Carlisle Indian School, **14**
Castile, Philando, 51
Chaney, James, 46
Chauvin, Derek, 52
Cherokee removal, 14–15
Chicago, 35–36, 48
Chinese Exclusion Act (1882), 7, 26
Chinese immigrants
    exclusion of, 7, 26
    stereotypes, 28
    violence against, **27**, 28
    West Coast expulsions of, 26
    westward expansion and, 27–28
Chinese Police Tax Act (California, 1862), 28
Christianity, conversion of Native Americans to, 13
Christian Register (newspaper), 18
Civilization Fund Act (1819), 13–14
Civil Rights Act (1866), 22
civil rights movement, 44–46
Civil War (1861–1865), 20–21
Clark, Kenneth, 39
Common Sense (Paine), 13
Confederate States of America, 20–21
COVID-19, 47
criminal justice system, 49–53
critical race theory (CRT), 51
Cullors, Patrisse, 53

Davis, John, 39
Declaration of Independence, 10, 18
Douglass, Frederick, 24
Dred Scott Supreme Court decision, 18–19
"driving while Black," 50–52

education
    critical race theory, 51
    of Native Americans, 13–14, **14**
    segregation in, 38–41, **41**
    1619 Project and, 55
    of slaves, 18
    systemic racism in, 48
Eisenhower, Dwight, 40, 45
Emancipation Proclamation, 20–21, **22**
Enlightenment, 10
Equal Justice Initiative, 29, 50
Executive Order 9066 (Roosevelt, 1942), 36

Executive Order 9981 (Truman, 1948), 32

Fifteenth Amendment (US Constitution), 22–23
Floyd, George, 52–53
Forrest, Nathan Bedford, 24
Freedom Riders, 44–45
Freedom Summer (1946), 46
Fugitive Slave Act (1793), 17

Garza, Alicia, 53
Goodman, Andrew, 46
Grant, Ulysses S., 25
Greaser Law (California, 1855), 16
Great Depression, 41–42
Great Migration, 34
Green, Ernest, 40–41, **41**

Hancock, John, 18
Harlem Hellfighters, 33, **33**
Hasen, Richard, 54
health care, 48–49
Hernandez, Kelly Lytle, 45
Hispanics
    arrests and beatings of, for wearing zoot suits, **43**, 43–44
    Bracero program, 45
    California gold strikes, 16
    deportations during Great Depression, 41–42
    Greaser Law (1855), 16
    Treaty of Guadalupe Hidalgo and, 15
housing, 48
Hume, David, 11

"I Have a Dream" speech (King), 45–46
Indian Removal Act (1830), 14–15
Invisible Empire. *See* Ku Klux Klan (KKK)

Japanese Americans and Japanese immigrants, during World War II, 8, 36–37, **37**
Jefferson, Thomas
    Native Americans and, 13
    as slave-owning writer of Declaration of Independence, 10, 18
Jenkins County, Georgia, 35
Jim Crow laws, 7, 25–27, 49–50
    See also segregation
Johnson, Andrew, 21, 22
Johnson, Lyndon, 41

Johnson, Samuel, 18
Justice Quarterly (journal), 28

Kant, Immanuel, 11
Kerner, Otto, 42
King, Andrew, 28
King, Martin Luther, Jr., 45–46
Knights of the White Camelia, 25
Ku Klux Klan (KKK)
    actions of, 24–25
    formation of, 23–24
    murders of civil rights workers, 46
    revival of, 31–32

law enforcement, 50–53
Lewis, Charles, 34
Lewis, John, 9
Lincoln, Abraham, 20–21, **22**
Linnaeus, Carl, 6, 10
Little Rock, Arkansas, 40–41, **41**
Little Rock Nine, 40–41, **41**
Los Angeles
    anti-Chinese riots, 28
    arrests and beatings of Hispanics
        for wearing zoot suits, **43**, 43–44
Los Angeles News, 28
Los Angeles Rams players, **56**
Louisiana Purchase, 14
lynchings of Blacks, 29–30, **31**, 34

Madison, James, 11, 18
March on Washington (1963), 45–46
Marshall, Thurgood, 39
Martin, Trayvon, 53
McLemore, Henry, 36
Mexican-American War, 15
Mexico
    Hispanic deportations to, during
        Great Depression, 41–42
    Mexican-American War, 15
    workers from, 45
military, Blacks in, 32, **33**
Minneapolis, Minnesota, 52–53
Montgomery, Alabama, 44–45
movies, 30–31

Nash, Diane, 26–27
National Academy of Medicine, 49
National Association for the
    Advancement of Colored People
    (NAACP)
    Brown v. Board of Education
        (1954), 38–39
    education lawsuits, 38
    lynchings and, 30
Native Americans, 13–15, **14**
Nature Human Behaviour (journal), 51
NBC News, 55–56
New York Evening Sun (newspaper), 34
New York Times (newspaper), 55
North Star (newspaper), 24

"Of National Characters" (Hume), 11
Onwuachi-Willig, Angela, 6–7
Operation Wetback, 45
Order of the Pale Faces, 25

Pacific Islanders. *See* Asians and
    Pacific Islanders
Paine, Thomas, 13
Palmieri, Elizabeth, 54
Pember, Mary Annette, 15
Perry, Barbara, 54–55
Perry, Benjamin F., 22
Persad, Jo, 48
Plessy, Homer, 26
Plessy v. Ferguson (1896), 26–27, 38
President's Committee on Civil
    Rights, 32
Proud Boys, 54
public opinion polls, 55–56

race
    as method of classifying people, 6, 10–11
    as social construct, 6–7
Radical Republicans, 22
Reconstruction (1865–1877), 21–23
Red Summer (Chicago), 35–36
repatriation drives, 41–42
Rogers, Will Ann, 16
Roosevelt, Franklin D., 36

Schwerner, Michael, 46
science and classification, 6, 10–11
Scott, Dred, 18–19
segregation
    education, 38–41, **41**
    Jim Crow laws, 7, 25–27, 49–50
    military, 32, **33**
    transportation, **25**
        Freedom Riders, 44–45
        Plessy v. Ferguson, 26–27, 28
        Supreme Court ruling on
        interstate bus, 44
Selma, Alabama, 46
Sentencing Project, 50
Silverstein, Jake, 55
Simmons, William J., 31–32
1619 Project (*New York Times*), 55
slaves and slavery, **12**
    Atlantic trade, 7, **8**, 11–12
    auctions, 12–13, 16
    at beginning of American
        Revolution, 18
    conditions, 12–13
    in Declaration of Independence, 18
    education of, 18
    Fugitive Slave Act, 17
    Lincoln and, 20–21
    plantation expansion, 16
    population (1790), 11
    population (1850), 16
    Turner rebellion, **17**, 17–18
    in US Constitution, 11

social construct, race as, 6–7
social media, 54
Southern Manifesto, 39–40
Southern Poverty Law Center, 54
Stop AAPI Hate, 47
Stop Asian Hate rally, **49**
systemic racism
    as normalized and rendered
        nearly invisible, 48
    public opinion about, 55–56
    roots of, 6–7
    widespread nature of, 48–49

Tacoma, Washington, 26
Taney, Roger B., 19
Taylor, Anh "Peng," 47
Tometi, Opal, 53
Trail of Tears, 14–15
transcontinental railroad, 27–28
transportation, **25**
    Freedom Riders, 44–45
    Plessy v. Ferguson, 26–27, 28
    Supreme Court ruling, 44
Treaty of Guadalupe Hidalgo (1848), 15
Truman, Harry S., 32
Trump, Donald, 53
Tulsa, Oklahoma, 35
Turner, Nat, **17**, 17–18

US Constitution, 11, 22–23
US Supreme Court
    Dred Scott decision, 18–19
    Plessy v. Ferguson, 26–27, 38
    segregation of transportation
        ruling, 44

voting rights
    Black codes, 23
    Fifteenth Amendment and, 22–23
    Freedom Summer, 46
    KKK and, 24–25
    Voting Rights Act (1964), 9

Wall Street Journal (newspaper), 55–56
Warren, Earl, 39
Washington, George, 11, 18
Washington, Jesse, 30
Washington Post (newspaper), 49–50
westward expansion
    Chinese immigrants and, 27–28
    relocation of Native Americans, 13, 14–15
White supremacists
    characteristics of current groups, 54–55
    Ku Klux Klan, 23–25, 31–32, 46
    lynchings by, 29–30, **31**, 34
    power of, at end of nineteenth
        century, 25
Williams, Eugene, 35
World War I, **33**, 33–34
World War II, 32, 36–37, **37**